Darwin
1869

THE FIRST YEAR IN PHOTOGRAPHS

DEREK PUGH

Darwin 1869: The First Year in Photographs
Text ©Derek Pugh 2018
Photographs: Joseph Brooks, Captain Samuel White Sweet; see State Library of South Australia and
Northern Territory Library.

Design and layout by Michael Pugh: michael.pugh@bigpond.com

Pugh, Derek: Author
Title: Darwin 1869: The First Year in Photographs
/Derek Pugh

ISBN: 9780648142133 : Printed—Paperback

Notes: Bibliographical references: see *Darwin 1869: The Second Northern Territory Expedition*, by Derek
Pugh.
Subjects:
Northern Territory of South Australia: Darwin—Palmerston—History
Aborigines: Wulna—Larrakia—Early contact—History—Billiamuk—Old Mira
Aboriginal–European relations
South Australian Colonisation: Exploration—Port Darwin—George Goyder—Dr Robert Peel—JWO
Bennett
Surveyors: Goyder—Mitchell—MacLachlan—Harvey—Smith—Knuckey—McMinn—Woods
Pioneers: Northern Territory—Social conditions
Diarists: George Woodroffe Goyder—William Hoare—George Dean—Dominic Daniel Daly
Ships: *Moonta—Gulnare—Kohinoor—Bengal—Gothenburg—Springbok*

Note: This book is a companion to *Darwin 1869: The Second Northern Territory Expedition* by Derek
Pugh (2018, ISBN 978-0-6481421-2-6). It is designed to primarily showcase the 1869 photographs of
Joseph Brooks and Captain Samuel Sweet, 150 years after settlement.

Front Cover: The Fort Point camp in late August or early September, 1869. The *Gulnare* is moored
            off the point. (Sweet SLSA B4650, stitched and colorised 2018.)

Contact:
derekpugh1@gmail.com
www.derekpugh.com.au

A catalogue record for this
book is available from the
National Library of Australia

Foreword

ONE HUNDRED AND FIFTY years ago, a motivated and professional team of surveyors and their support staff arrived in Darwin Harbour to measure the land and divide it into allotments already sold by the South Australian government. This was the second attempt by the South Australians to establish a colony on the north coast and, under the leadership of the Surveyor-General, George Goyder, the work was done at an astonishing rate. This book is a summary of the story published simultaneously with my book *Darwin 1869: The Second Northern Territory Expedition.* This

Brooks used a stereographic camera which allowed a 3D view of the image when looked at through a viewer of paired lenses (SLSA B11601).

Joseph Brooks, the expedition photographer and draftsman (SLSA B16791-15).

Samuel White Sweet, Captain of the *Gulnare* and amateur photographer (Anon. PRG 742-5-95).

Sweet's photographs can often be identified by a small anchor scratched onto the plate before printing (Street, 1869, detail of SLSA B4647).

book celebrates the work of two men in particular, whose photographs allow us to peer into the lives of our first settlers.

JOSEPH BROOKS arrived in Adelaide at the age of nine. He became a draftsman with the South Australian Department of Survey and Crown Lands in 1864 and was chosen by Goyder to join the Northern Territory Expedition when he was 21 years old. As well as being a draftsmen, Brooks was the official photographer for the expedition until he left the settlement in September with Goyder on the *Gulnare*. He used a stereographic camera that took two images which could be seen in 3D when used with a viewer of paired lenses. In later years he moved to New South Wales for a further career in surveying and then took up astronomy, travelling the Pacific Ocean to chase solar eclipses. He died of Bright's disease in 1918 in Woollahra, aged 70.

CAPTAIN SAMUEL WHITE SWEET was a keen amateur photographer and he was able to help Brooks take the official photographs as well as take his own that he could then sell to the public back in Adelaide. As Brooks's drafting duties became more time consuming, Sweet took over much of the role of 'official' photographer.

Sweet's photographs can often be identified by a small anchor-shaped scratch etched onto the plate before printing.

Captain Sweet brought the *Gulnare* five times from Adelaide to Port Darwin but in October

1821 she hit a reef near the Vernon Islands while carrying telegraph line equipment to the Roper River. She was able to limp back to Port Darwin, but Government Resident Douglas, who found her slow and unwieldy, was delighted to condemn the little ship. She was stripped of anything useful and left to rot on the beach below Fort Hill. Her masts were reclaimed, and were later strapped to the side of the *Springbok* to take south. Captain Sweet returned to Adelaide to captain the *Wallaroo*, carting coal for the Black Diamond Line, until she ran aground in a storm in 1875. He then retired from the sea and opened a photography business off Rundell Street, Adelaide. He was one of South Australia's most prominent documentary photographers through the 1870s to January 1886, when he collapsed and died near Riverton, South Australia, apparently of sunstroke. He was survived by Elizabeth Tilly, with whom he had had four daughters and five sons.

Since both Brooks and Sweet left the colony on September 28, there was no photographer in Palmerston until Sweet's return at the end of January, 1870. Most of the images in this book were therefore made between February 5 and September 28, 1869. They are precious—Darwin is unusual in that it is the only pre-Federation Australian capital to have been photographed from the very beginning.

Indigenous Australians should be aware that images of people who are deceased are necessarily a part of this publication.

Derek Pugh, Darwin, June 2018

The Second Northern Territory Expedition

CAPTAIN THOMAS BARNESON ordered the *Moonta's* sails to be furled and the anchor to be dropped. Fort Point looked green and lush in the afternoon sun. He could see the plateau running northwards towards Point Emery and on their right the small Fort Hill, a peninsula in its own right, seemed to stand guard over the eastern entrance to the huge Darwin Harbour behind it. Barneson had two maps: one drawn by Lieutenant Stokes of the *Beagle* in 1839; the other by JWO Bennett, drawn only a few years earlier as part of his duties on the First Northern Territory Expedition. The name Darwin had been given to the harbour by Stokes and Commander Wickham after their old shipmate of five years, Charles Darwin. It was before his rise to fame—Darwin never actually visited the harbour himself.

The *Moonta* was low in the water. Her holds were packed tight with stores of every description and livestock, including horses, cattle, dogs and chickens. As the anchor fell, the *Moonta's* decks were crowded while her passengers eagerly scanned the shoreline of what was to become their new home. Captain Barneson and the *Moonta* had been chartered just months before by the Surveyor-General of South Australia, George Woodroffe Goyder, to transport the Second Northern Territory Expedition to the Northern Territory of South Australia. They were there to ensure South Australia's second attempt to establish a colony was more successful than the first.

Goyder's expedition included nearly 140 officers and men. They were to survey and mark out the site of a new city to be called Palmerston. Sailing from Adelaide a few days after Christmas in 1868, they had taken five weeks to travel around the west coast of Australia to Port Darwin. The long journey had been dull and boring, but the survey teams amused themselves with boxing matches, music and ribald shows, and by writing a small newspaper, the *Moonta Herald*. Some of the younger surveyors and cadets also prepared for and sat surveying exams. Goyder wrote that John Brooking, who also played the flute, did the best in them; Chris Giles and Charles Sprigg scraped through, but Thomas Bee was 'utterly ignorant of the theoretical branch of the profession'; and Alex McKay was a 'little deficient in the practical application of the rules'.

Some of the men in the expedition already had experience of the Northern Territory. They had been members of the First Northern Territory Expedition, which had set up on Escape Cliffs* at the mouth of the Adelaide River, in 1864. Poorly led by Colonel Boyle Travers Finniss, the expedition failed dismally and after two years the men were recalled to Adelaide. They left behind several of their number— dead through illness or accident by drowning. One was speared by local Aborigines. Several Wulna tribesmen also paid the final price.

In all, 14 men of the first expedition had signed up for their second. Making the most of the experience on the long voyage north, they were happy to tell stories to the wide-eyed greenhorns:

'An old victim of Northern Territory enterprise advises his friends to make preparations for the mosquitos before landing, assuring them as a fact that they have been known to get on a log and bark, and a great many of them weigh a pound.' (Issue 1, Moonta Herald, *1869.)*

---

* For more on this story, see Pugh, 2018: *Escape Cliffs: The First Northern Territory Expedition, 1864–66.*

Now the newcomers would be able to see this isolated part of Australia for themselves. George Goyder recorded their arrival in his journal: 'The *Moonta*', he wrote, 'arrived at Port Darwin in afternoon of 5th Feby (*sic*) 1869 and came to anchor at 3.15 pm opposite Fort Pt.'

Twenty-two of the expedition were then rowed to the beach with Captain Barneson and Surveyor-General Goyder. They included the expedition doctor, Robert Peel, several of the officers: Mitchell, Woods, McMinn, MacLachlan, Berry, and Hardy; and Schultz and son, the naturalists. They had a quick look around and Goyder chose a few likely places he could start the well diggers searching for water. They also needed wood for fires, timber to start constructing huts, a store house, yards for the animals, and living spaces to be cleared of the bush. The teams were readied for an early morning start the next day. Some of the men remained on board to start unloading the animals and the mountain of stores. In the end, even the *Moonta's* wheel house was unloaded and used for accommodation in the camp.

The next day was a Saturday and Goyder and Captain Barneson were up early. By 5 am they were in a dinghy being rowed along the coast looking for the best anchorages and fresh water because, with so many men and animals, fresh water was essential. They found it seeping from the rocks onto the beach, trickling down from the plateau in seasonal drains and, further around, in a small creek which flowed over a waterfall and through a gully into the sea. There was plenty of water, at least for a time, but the well-diggers, Donald McAulay, Martin Moyse, and Francis Bennett, were still sent out with 'tube-wells and other tools'. Dr Peel took a team back to the gully and cleared a path up through the bush and dug there. His well became known as Peel's Well, and the gully as Doctor's Gully, as it still is today.

Goyder was, at first, a reluctant leader of the expedition. He had been pressured by the 'Goyder Agitation' of powerful members of Adelaide society, until finally he conceded. After negotiating a generous payment and reward system, he left behind his wife, Frances, and nine children who went to England for the interim. (Sadly, Goyder never saw Frances again as she died from an accidental overdose of sleeping pills.)

Goyder was not known as 'Little Energy' for nothing. He drove himself and his men hard. They were there to do a job—the surveyors and their teams were being paid well and there were bonuses each month for any extra square miles surveyed. They were in a hurry, and not just because they wanted to go home. The South Australian Government's plan to settle the north had been designed to be at no cost to tax payers. They had sold the land, unseen, un-located and unsurveyed, to investors in Adelaide and London back in 1864, raising £70,000. This had funded the first expedition. However, they were contracted to provide the land within five years and most of that time, and most of the money raised, had already been wasted. The investors were angry. The government was concerned they would be forced to pay them back.

Only Goyder could save them, said the *Adelaide Advertiser*, by getting the land surveyed and ensuring the investors had their parcels of land—a half-acre town allotment and a 320-acre rural plot—before the end of 1869.

Goyder took control and was ready to go within two months. The *Moonta* was loaded and a second ship, the *Sea Ripple*, bought to transport tools and equipment, and houses in frame.

On arrival at Port Darwin, Goyder was puzzled by the empty waters. The *Sea Ripple* should have been there already. Its loss could be a serious blow to the colony. Goyder worried while he monitored their supplies, and considered rationing the food.

The camp was situated on the southern part of the Port Darwin peninsula in a saddle between Fort Hill and the forested plateau of the peninsula. The saddle seemed cooler than the plateau. It became known as the 'depot', 'Fort Point' or simply the 'camp'.

The *Moonta* was unloaded and the camp organised within a few days. The cattle and horses were led out to find fresh grass, the tents pitched and the prefabricated huts put together. Several buildings were constructed from bush timber, like the government store, which was 15 metres long by 6 metres wide and roofed with corrugated iron sheets and tree bark. A cement-making kiln was constructed, burning coral and shells to make mortar.

William Hayes, the gardener, started planting at Doctor's Gully. He was helped by Robert Burton and Ned Tuckwell, who went on a salvage mission to the old Escape Cliffs site at the Adelaide River mouth to bring back anything useful they could find. This included bananas, pineapples, arrowroot, and other plants for the garden.

Goyder was pleased:

'Port Darwin, February 20, 1869

'The Surveyor-General begs to thank the officers and men of the party for their ready and constant attendance to keep up proper discipline during the voyage and good fellowship amongst themselves. He also wishes to express the satisfaction he feels at the progress made since the arrival of the ship at this port and trusts to be able to give all a day's holiday after the cargo has been landed and stored, when they will assemble to wish the captain and officers' health and a speedy and safe voyage home.

G.W. GOYDER.'

The *Moonta* stayed a few more weeks. Barneson was able to explore the harbour with Goyder in the ship's boat. Together they searched West Arm, South Arm and East Arm for sites suitable for ships landing. At East Arm they met up with Alexander Mitchell, who had led his survey team overland to mark out roads and begin the early surveys. Sites for the new towns of Southport and Virginia were identified.

Back at Fort point the plateau was ready for survey. The town plan was based on a template drawn by Joseph Brooks, which followed the rectangular grid pattern used in Adelaide. Goyder merely had to adjust the grid according to the topography of the Palmerston peninsula, which has the sea on three sides. He needed to plan for government spaces, a central business district, port facilities, warehouse areas, parklands and public squares, schools, cemeteries, commercial areas, roads, and light industrial spaces. There were over 1,400 land orders sold in London and Adelaide that had to be filled. Most of the half-acre blocks had to fit between the public spaces and the roads. Goyder's original plan squeezed on 999 town allotments in an area of 1,015 hectares. His map shows how crowded the peninsula suddenly became.

Goyder named most of the streets after his senior surveyors. He also ran a green reserve down the western coast that he called the 'Public Esplanade'. Using Brooks's city plan template, Goyder designed the city of Darwin on the morning of February 11, 1869. Its moment in history took up only a few words of his diary:

'Thursday 11th Parties proceeded to shore as usual at 7 a.m. Designed plan of township and set draftsmen to work preparing 6 copies for use of Surveyor. Invalids better. Proceeded to shore. Gave necessary instructions for work to be carried out and started ... to examine Eastern Arm.'

The towns of Southport and Virginia were planned in the same way—with fewer adjustments because of their more open topography.

Once Goyder had identified the port area, and the locations of the inland towns and the major geography of the country, he organised the expedition into three groups he called 'double parties' because they were led by two first class surveyors: George MacLachlan and Gilbert McMinn; Arthur Smith and William Harvey; and Alfred Woods and Alexander Mitchell. They were appointed to separate areas starting from near Palmerston and from the South Arm and East Arm of the harbour. Each double party of 32 men was divided into two single parties of 16 men. They were then split into groups of seven, with two left over as camp keepers or draftsmen. The work units were then allocated 33 square miles of land to survey each month. This was to be done on standard pay but for every extra square mile above that the surveyors would get a bonus of five shillings and one penny. The work was tough and exhausting in the tropical heat and insects. They would regularly begin by candlelight before dawn, and finish after dark, and the rate of survey was huge. More than 30,000 acres a week (12,000 hectares) could be achieved. The entire area of 665,866 acres (over 1000 square miles, or 269,675 hectares) extending 58 miles inland, was sliced up into 320- and 160-acre blocks. Landmarks, used by the local inhabitants for millennia, were given foreign names, and future towns, roads and reserves were carefully plotted onto paper.

Goyder was becoming increasingly concerned about the *Sea Ripple*. Eyes strained to catch a

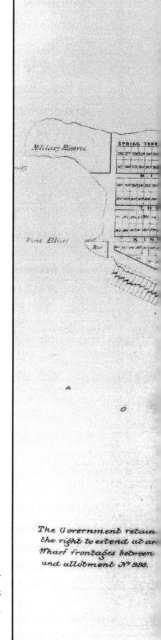

An 1870 plan of Palmerston signed by George Goyder. Nearly 1000 allotments were squeezed onto the peninsula. (NTL, Map_8-185a_Palmerston).

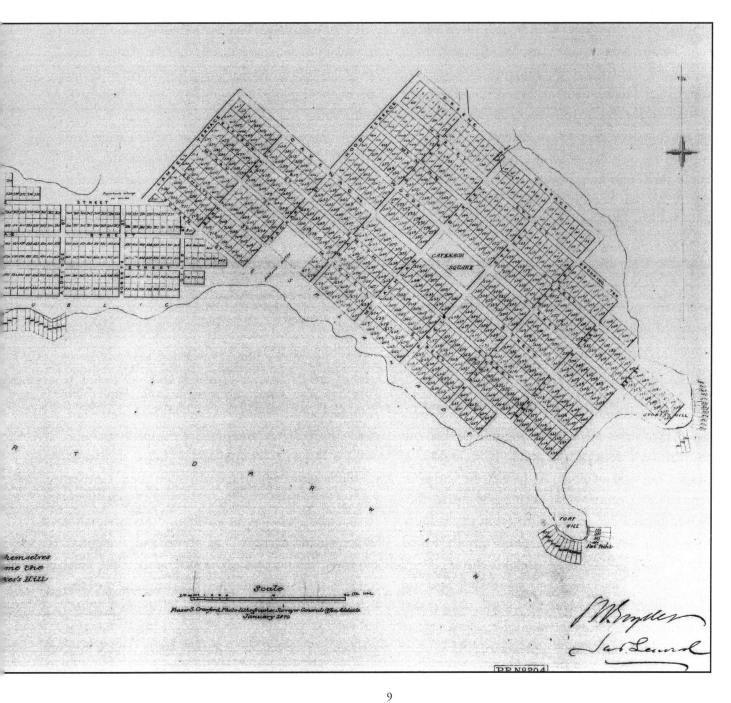

glimpse of her, but days went by and there was no sign. Finally, seven weeks after the *Moonta* arrived, sails were sighted on the horizon. Not the *Sea Ripple*, but a schooner named the *Gulnare*, bought to replace the *Sea Ripple* when she was found to be unseaworthy. She was loaded with huts in kit form, iron roofing sheets, tools, food supplies and a small one-horsepower steam launch named the *Midge* that became invaluable in transporting men and equipment down to Southport. The *Gulnare's* captain was Samuel White Sweet. He would sail her back and forth from Adelaide to Darwin five times over the next few years and, as an amateur (later professional) photographer, he could help, and add to, the work done by the official photographer, Joseph Brooks. We have these two men to thank for the early photographs of the colony.

Throughout March and April, the survey teams based themselves at bush camps and travelled out to their day's work each morning. Huge areas were pegged out and mapped. As a rule, the surveyors returned to a central camp each night but, as they moved further out, they had to camp in the bush. Eventually, the cook and a camp minder would move the central camp to catch up to them.

In May, Goyder started a month long field trip that enabled him to visit all the survey camps as well as explore new country westwards of the place where Fred Litchfield had found gold in 1865.

The naturalists, Fred Schultz and his son Alfred, accompanied Goyder on a horse cart because they could not ride horses. Together they collected 8,000 specimens of plants and animals and sent them back to the South Australian Museum.

Goyder visited the camp at Fred's Pass in late May. This was run by Alfred Woods and Alexander Mitchell but when Goyder's party arrived, the only men in the camp were John William Olgivie Bennett and William Guy. Bennett was a 23-year-old experienced draftsman who had been on the Escape Cliffs expedition. He had developed a keen interest in the local Aboriginal tribe, the Wulna, and had even learned their language. In fact, he was working on a dictionary of Wulna place names and vocabulary when Goyder arrived.

Goyder did not trust the local Aborigines. Port Darwin was on Larrakia land and their neighbours, the Wulna, had already had some poor experiences from the settlers of Escape Cliffs four and five years earlier, and he had heard that some of them wanted revenge. To feel safer, Goyder had ordered his men to travel armed and ready to defend themselves at all times. They were also to keep their distance and refuse trades or gifts. However, Bennett was interested in the culture of the locals, was learning their language and appears to have been close to a few individuals. As a result, he did not follow Goyder's rules. When Goyder arrived at Fred's Pass he found Bennett at work, unarmed, at the drafting table and Guy cooking, also unarmed. Goyder had:

'... personally remonstrated with him for his persistent familiarity with the natives, and had written a special memorandum upon the subject.'

Goyder was annoyed because Bennett 'continued to trust the natives implicitly' and considered himself perfectly safe. Moreover, those around Bennett, like Guy, also thought they were safe because of Bennett's influence. His annoyance and warnings proved to be prophetic.

Goyder had been determined to remain on good relations with the local tribes and thought the best way was to keep them a distance. In these early days, the Larrakia may have thought of the white men as visitors rather than settlers, and their land-clearing and well sinking must have seemed strange, and their habit of leaving lines of painted survey pegs through the bush highly eccentric.

The settlers were actually welcomed by two young men, Billiamuk and Umballa, who paddled out to the *Moonta* the day after she arrived. 'They did not seem frightened at all' wrote George Deane, which suggested that they were already familiar with Europeans. They proved this by showing they already knew a few English words. Then, when they were invited on board, they sang 'Old John Brown' and 'Ole Virginny' to the astonished white men. They had visited the first expedition at Escape Cliffs, probably when James Manton was in charge, and had clearly spent enough time with them to build up the confidence of familiarity. They were happy to show the new-comers around, and even guided them to Doctor's Gully for water, although it was a site they had already found.

Billiamuk became a well-known character around town and, later, he and several others were taken to Adelaide so they could see the power of the white colonisers. He also interceded in fights between the settlers and armed Larrakia men, which probably saved both expeditioners and Larrakia men from certain injury. There is a suburb in modern Darwin named after him: Bellamack.

The broad implications of setting up a new colony in northern Australia was not lost on Goyder. He knew he was surveying tribal lands, mostly that of the Larrakia and Wulna. He personally saw very few Aborigines when he was in the bush but he was always of the opinion that they were there watching him, unseen. He showed some understanding when he wrote:

'We were in what to them appeared unauthorised and unwarranted occupation of their country ... Territorial rights are strictly observed by the natives ... even a chief of one tribe will neither hunt upon nor remove anything from the territory of another without first obtaining permission ... it is scarcely to be wondered at if, when opportunity is allowed them, they should resent such acts upon the perpetrators.'

He therefore reminded the expeditioners that they were never to be out by themselves and they should always be armed. The surveyors would peer down their theodolites with pistols in their belts and the axemen would carry carbine rifles with their axes. Goyder's rules also stated that only senior staff were allowed to converse with Aborigines but only on special occasions and never after dark. He banned the survey parties from 'employing' Aborigines to fetch wood or water and they were not to be given food unless they were sick or there was authorised barter. This is despite the friendship of Billiamuk and others, and some Larrakia men already proving to be a great help in the first few days after their arrival, bringing huge sheets of *Eucalyptus* bark for roofing material. Nevertheless, very soon Goyder banned the locals from approaching within 18 metres of the camp and had a fence constructed around it. Tensions grew. On one night the settlers heard activity in the surrounding bush. Fearful of attack, Goyder rostered the cadets and draftsmen into a night guard.

In mid-April, a friendly, half-expected face appeared. An old man named Mira, from the Adelaide River region, turned up and was delighted to reacquaint himself with his friends from Escape Cliffs days, like John Bennett and Harrison Packard. Mira had mediated on behalf of the first expeditioners a number of times and had lived at the Escape Cliffs camp after the Europeans had abandoned it.

Mira was an elder of the Wulna people and he was accompanied by several of his tribe and two Malay fishermen. The Malays were survivors of a ship which was wrecked two years earlier and Goyder was pleased to organise transport back to Kupang for them on the *Gulnare*. He was also happy to give the Wulna tribesmen food as a reward for their 'humanity'. Mira became a useful and frequent visitor to the camp from then on and would sometimes guide exploring parties and mediate between the whites and any armed groups of Aborigines they met.

But these friendly Aborigines were not around in the Fred's Pass camp on May 24. John Bennett, still ignoring the Surveyor-General's orders to be armed at all times, and William Guy were alone in the camp when they were attacked by several armed warriors. Guy was wounded in his buttocks, though not fatally. John Bennett, however, was hit by several spears, one of which entered his chest. Doctor Peel removed a 22-centimetre piece of it in an operation back at Fort Point when the wounded men were finally brought in. However, Bennett died the next day and was buried on Fort Hill on May 29. His grave, which he later shared with a cook named Richard Hazard who died of a 'lung complaint' in August, remained undisturbed until 1965 when Fort Hill was removed to make way for an iron ore facility. Nowadays, their grave can be found in a central part of the Jingili Cemetery.

Goyder was still on his field trip when Bennett was murdered. Coincidentally, his party had climbed Mount Bennett that same day. It had been named after Bennett by Fred Litchfield during his explorations in 1865.

Alarmed by the murder, when Goyder returned to Fort Point he ordered the survey teams to contract their camps and be more careful to follow the rules. He wasn't surprised by the attack and understood it to be in revenge for the murders committed at Escape Cliffs but he refused to be drawn into reprisals against innocent Aborigines in an attempt to avoid escalating the problem.

The surveys were nearly complete in any case. By the end of June, groups of men were gathering at Southport to await their return to Fort Point by the *Midge*. They spent their spare time hunting geese at Goose Lagoon and panning for gold at Tumbling Waters, on the Blackmore River.

By the middle of the dry season, the men at Fort Point were having problems getting enough water. Charles Miller, the engineer for the *Midge*, had a clever idea. He removed the boiler of his little boat and set it up as a still. He could then boil as much as 150 gallons of seawater a day and collect fresh water from the end of a long cooling pipe. With new wells dug and the desalination plant working, their water problems were solved, although the loss of steam power to the *Midge* must have been keenly felt.

Since their days spent sailing around the coast on the *Moonta*, the men had entertained themselves by performing for each other in concerts led by Dr Robert Peel. As the surveys were coming to an end and more and more men returned to Fort Point, the number of performers and the size of their audiences grew. Dr Peel organised the construction of a theatre, known as the Theatre Royal. On successive Saturday nights, the men put on performances in the theatre. Goyder said they were mostly 'pretty good', although on one occasion he walked out, unable to cope with the blasphemy of the performers and an 'imperious remark' that was 'uncalled for'. The Saturday night performances were immensely popular and the doctor's assistant, William Hoare, recorded that he could often hear men rehearsing.

By September all the surveying was complete, including 150,000 additional acres the government had ordered at the last minute. The surveyors and their teams thought their time in the north was coming to an end. But the only ship available to take them home was the schooner, *Gulnare*, which carried only 35 passengers. Goyder asked for volunteers to stay in the camp. The government wanted it inhabited to protect it until they could organise a government resident and settlers to move in and take over, which wouldn't happen until the next year.

Some were happy to stay—they would remain on salary and their tasks wouldn't be too onerous— or so they thought. Others resented the extra time in the north.

On September 28, Goyder left the settlement on the *Gulnare*, never to return. He took with him the surveyors McMinn, Mitchell, Woods, A. Smith, E. Smith, Knuckey and Thomas; draftsmen Berry and Brooks; and about 30 other members of the expedition.

Fort Point, Port Darwin, 1869. An oil painting by WW Hoare of the main camp of the Northern Territory Survey Expedition, published in *The Illustrated Australian News* on 22 May, 1869 (SLSA B1048).

His report was completed on September 27. In just under nine months they had surveyed:

> *1st Principal town at Fort point, 999 half-acre allotments, roads, parks, reserves and cemetery reserves, totalling 2,506½ acres.*
> *2nd Township on the River Blackmore: 498½ acres, including roads, reserves, parks and cemetery.*
> *3rd Township on the Elizabeth, a total of 628½ acres.*
> *4th Township at Fred's Pass , a total of 794½ acres.*
> *5th 1,708 blocks each 320 acres.*
> *6th 208 blocks each 160 acres.*
> *7th 330 blocks of irregular area 73,964 acres.*
> *8th Roads, 7,554 acres.*
> *9th Reserves, 80 acres,*
> *Total 665,886 acres.*

Those left behind at Fort point now fell under the leadership of Dr Robert Peel.

Peel was not a popular leader but he was charged with keeping the men working, even when most of them felt their jobs were complete. Their major projects were the back-breaking road works up to the plateau and completion of the government stables. Peel was already disliked, because from the early days he was often unavailable to the sick—preferring to explore the country on horseback, or go hunting. And worse, there had been arguments over his unequal distribution of alcohol:

> *'For some days past there has been frightful dissatisfaction in camp, the chief cause being the rations, which are certainly very bad, and*

the other reason being connected with the Doctor and his companions' use of medical comforts. The Doctor has often expressed the opinion that spirituous liquors in this tropical climate were bad for the men, but this seems strangely inconsistent with his own practice. He seems to imagine that men when worn out with fatigue only need lots of physicking, and that wines, beer, &c, are only necessary to a medical man after his arduous duties.' (Register, *March 29, 1870*).

But, Peel wrote:

'It is very difficult under existing circumstances to know how to act; the majority of the men are so dissatisfied and disappointed at the non-arrival of a steamer, for it was expected that they would have been in Adelaide at Christmas time. The men also considered that the agreement they signed was binding only up to the completion of the land survey.'

Relationships went from bad to worse. On December 28, the anniversary of their departure from Adelaide, the men felt they deserved a holiday but were ordered to work. They started out, but the mood quickly soured and they down-tooled. It was the first strike in the Northern Territory and Peel had to capitulate. Then, on New Year's Eve, some revellers stoned Peel's roof, making a frightful racket on the tin.

Tensions rose in the colony. Tempers grew short. The camp was interminably dull and the work tiresome. George Deane and John Roberts got into a scuffle over a stool Deane used for his meteorological duties. Deane came off second best, dislocating his little finger.

Every day they scanned the horizon and willed the arrival of a ship, but it was not until late January 1870 that the *Gulnare* came into view. With it was the *Kohinoor*, full of new settlers, the wives of some of the expeditioners, and even some of their children. A few members of the expedition found on-going employment in the colony and stayed as their colleagues returned to Adelaide. They were therefore among the first settlers of the new colony of Palmerston.

Palmerston had its name changed in 1911, and the city has been called Darwin ever since. The members of the Second Northern Territory Expedition are remembered in names of streets or land features in and around the city. There is a Goyder Road, and Dr Peel is remembered in Peel Street and Peel's Well; the names of Smith, Knuckey, Bennett, Harvey, Mitchell, Woods, McMinn, Mc Lachlan and Daly Streets will all be familiar to visitors of the city centre. Further out they will come across Brooking Creek, Knuckey's Lagoon, Lake Bennett, McMinn's Lagoon, Daly Waters, Daly River, and a hundred other sites. They are not the original names of those places, but it's what the settlers and their successors have called them for the past one-and-a-half centuries.

Personnel of the Second Northern Territory Expedition, 1869

Surveyor-General, Leader	George Woodroffe Goyder
Surgeon, 2nd in charge	Dr Robert Peel (also the leader after Goyder's departure).
Surgeon's assistant, artist and diarist.	William Webster Hoare
Draftsmen	John WO Bennett, Edwin Stow Berry, Alexander Ringwood, Wentworth Marmeduke Hardy, Joseph Brooks (the official photographer)
Accountant/Postmaster	James M Lambell
Botanist/Assistant Botanist	Frederick Schultze/John Alfred Schultze
Carpenter.	William Barlow
Storekeeper and clerk	Hugh C McCallum

First-class surveyors	Arthur Henry Smith, Alfred Thomas Woods, William Harvey, Alexander James Mitchell, Gilbert Rotherdale McMinn, George Gailbraith MacLachlan
Second-class surveyors	Richard Randall Knuckey, Joseph Middlemore Thomas, William Whitfield Mills, Edwin Mitchell, Stephen King (jnr), Dominic Daniel Daly
Cadets	Charles Newton Greene, Christopher Giles (Jnr), Harrison Daniel Packard, John Sherlock Brooking, Alexander M McKay, Thomas Bee, Charles WL Sprigg, George S Aldridge, David L Beetson, Phillip Henry Burdon, John F Roberts, Charles H Wells
Coxswain	James Burton

Surveyor-General 's staff	Robert Charles Burton, William G Holland, Henry Hemming, Arthur Hicks, Frank Wighton Hood, Alick Kennedy, William Rowe (Jnr), Walter L Samson, Edward (Ned) Tuckwell.	**Teamsters**	Michael Bennett, Charles Fry, Robert Hayball, Peter Krüss, Patrick Molloy, james Oborn, Robert Price, Charles J Palmer, David Wilson
Cooks	North Smith, Henry Bosworth, David Donley, Richard Hazard, Charles Spencely, Alexander McKenzie, Adam Gaire, Thomas Stevens, Charles Laycock	**Storeman, camp keeper**	John G Nottage
		Well sinkers	Donald McAulay, E Martin Moyse, Terence McIntyre
Stock managers	Robert Charles Beard, William Barrett Rowe (Snr)	**Axemen and general hands, 'camp keepers' etc.**	George A Armstrong, Job Austin, George Bayfield, Francis John Bennett, Robert W Barrow, Robert Collard, William Collett, Walter Dalwood, James H Douglas, George Price Deane, Joseph A Ewart, Michael Francis, William John Farrant, Donald Fraser, William Guy, John Gerald, Richard Hinton, Richard Austin Horn, G Hughes, William Houston, Dennis Heir, Henry Irwin, David Johnson, Michael Keiley, Heinrich Ralfs Krüss, Patrick Kelly, George Kersley, John London, Cornelius Lowther, Charles J Lines, Richard J Loveday, James McPherson, Thomas Neate, George Richards, James Robinson, Michael C and John Ryan, Robert R Stevenson, John W Smith, Grosvenor Samuel Walters, Frederick Willson, William Guy, Wilhelm L Homeyer,
Farrier and blacksmith	William John Gepp		
Smith	Thomas Sayer		
Gardener	William B Hayes		
Carpenter	Benjamin Wells		
Chainmen	James H Aldridge, Thomas Cherry, Henry Cornish, William Henry Edwards, William Fisher, Matthew Houston, Arthur F Lines, William C Musgrave, Martin Burke, John Harrison Packard, William Plaisted		
Trenchers	William Stanborough, William Gunn, Thomas Sutherland Horn, Patrick Healey, John Lowther, Thomas Loveday, Alfred Warren		

Reproduced from *Darwin 1869: The Second Northern Territory Expedition* (Derek Pugh, 2018).

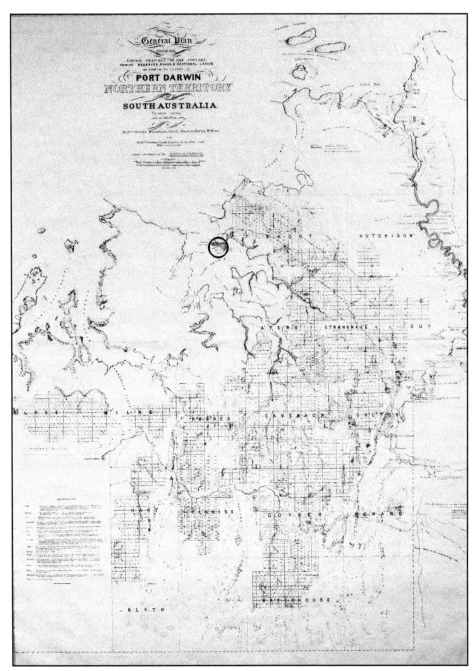

Map showing the full extent of the surveys undertaken in 1869. The dark ring just above the centre of the map indicates the Palmerston survey area shown in the map on Page 9 (NTL, Rare_Map_67c-3-2).

The photographs

Above: The *Moonta* was a three-masted sailing ship of 656 tonnes, built in Maine, USA in 1847. By 1868 she was already elderly, working as an inter-colony trader in Australia. After 1864, most of her time in Australia was spent carting coal between Newcastle and Wallaroo but in 1868 she was chosen by Goyder, and chartered by the South Australian Government, to take him and the surveyors to Port Darwin. On arrival, the *Moonta* was unloaded and stripped of everything useful to the colony. Even the wheelhouse was removed to become accommodation on shore (Anon., c1869, SLSA B11922).

Left: The 152-tonne *Gulnare* was a Canadian-built, ex-Caribbean slaver, bought by the South Australian Government for £1700 to replace the *Sea Ripple*, a ship Goyder had organised in Melbourne but which had been found to be unseaworthy. Captain Samuel Sweet brought the *Gulnare* to Port Darwin twice in 1869 and three more times in subsequent years, until she hit a reef after the Vernon Islands, while carrying telegraph line equipment to the Roper River. Sweet managed to sail her back to Port Darwin but Government Resident Douglas, who never liked the little ship, was delighted to condemn her. She was then stripped of anything useful and left to rot on the beach below Fort Hill. This photograph shows the *Gulnare* moored off the Southport jetty (Sweet, 1871, SLSA B840).

Ship "Moonta" arrived at Pt Darwin on afternoon of 5th Feby 1869 and came to anchor at 3.15 p.m. opposite Fort Pt. Two boats were at once lowered and put off for land; the first containing the Surveyor General, Doctor, Capt Barneson, Messrs Mitchell, Woods, McMinn, McLachlan, Berry, Hardy, Schultze, and the following men:– Collett, Edwards, and a seaman of the "Moonta." The second boat contained R. Burton, Packwell, Wm Rowe Senr, Wm Rowe junr, D. McAulay, A. Kennedy, J. Lowther, C. J. Palmer, & S. Loveday. Upon the return of the party to ship

In his journal, Goyder recorded the arrival time of the *Moonta* as 3.15 pm on February 5, 1869. The journal is now in the Northern Territory Archives in Darwin (NTAS 3732).

A montage of portraits of officers of the Northern Territory Expedition. These portraits originally come from a cardboard photo board donated to the South Australian State Library by Goyder's granddaughter, Barbara Kerr. It originally held small photos of 33 of the officers, but missing from the original frame are the portraits of Accountant Lambell, Draughtsman Hardy, and Cadets Greene, Beetson, Robert, Dye and Holland. Note that John Bennett was wrongly labelled 'Burnett' (Anon. 1868, SLSA B16791).

Above: The Larrakia traditionally own all of the land from the Cox peninsula in the west to Gunn Point in the north, Adelaide River in the east and to the Manton River in the far south. Many Larrakia moved to seasonal fringe camps around the edge of Palmerston for much of the first few years. Neither the white newcomers nor the Larrakia could possibly have imagined the long-lasting effects their arrival would have on all the tribes of the Northern Territory (Anon., c1870, SLSA B11948).

Right: The day after arriving at Port Darwin two Larrakia men, Billiamuk and Umballa, paddled out to the *Moonta* and astonished the expeditioners because they already knew a few English words and they could sing 'Old John Brown' and 'Ole Virginny' to the white men. They had learned English when the first expedition was at Escape Cliffs, probably when Manton was in charge. They agreed to show the newcomers where to get fresh water and they led them to Doctor's Gully, which Goyder had already found the day before. They became well known characters about town and were curiosities to southerners. The surveyor, Dominic Daly, and the explorers John McKinlay and John Davis took them to Adelaide in 1870, supposedly to impress them with the obvious power of white people, and thereby convincing all Aborigines to desist from hostilities. They were returned to Darwin at government expense on the 'grounds of humanity'. In this later photo by Inspector Paul Foelsche, Billiamuk is about 30 years old and wears a kangaroo-teeth head-dress. He was employed by Foelsche on occasion as a police tracker. He lived in Darwin and its surrounds for many years, dying in his sixties sometime after 1912 (Foelsche, 1880, SA Museum AA96).

George Woodroffe Goyder (1826-1898), the Surveyor General of South Australia, was pushed by public pressure into accepting the leadership role of the second expedition. Known as 'Little Energy', he did so under his own terms, agreeing only if he had control of the logistics of the expedition, recruitment, and even the power to decide on the right site for the settlement. He also negotiated a bonus of £3,000 for himself and productivity bonuses for the surveyors (Anon., c1875, SLSA B14656).

Above: An unidentified survey team posing with their equipment. It is possible this is Richard Knuckey's team because in the centre, holding his hat, is John Bennett. Bennett was a senior draftsmen who was with Knuckey's team at Fred's Pass, working on his vocabulary list of Aboriginal words and place names, when he was speared on May 24, 1869. He died on May 28th, after a 22-centimetre piece of the spear was removed from his lung cavity. He was buried the following day on Fort Hill with a Church of England ceremony (Brooks, 1869, SLSA B11599).

A survey party sits with their surveying tools. Seated on the left is John Bennett (Brooks, 1869, SLSA B11603).

Above: The grave of JWO Bennett and Richard Hazard, Fort Hill 1869 (Brooks, SLSA B56584) and, *Below*: as photographed by Brian T Manning in 1958.

John William Olgivie Bennett (1845–1869) was a talented draftsman and cartographer who had been a member of the First Northern Territory Expedition. He grew to respect the local Aborigines greatly and learned the Wulna language. The vocabulary list Bennett was compiling at the time of his death was published in 1869 as *Vocabulary of Woolner District Dialect, Adelaide River, Northern Territory*. A 30-page copy of this was owned and much annotated by Inspector Paul Foelsche in subsequent years (Anon., 1868, SLSA B16791/16).

An unidentified surveying team standing with their tools. Each man is armed with a revolver. Goyder personally saw very few Aborigines when he was in the bush, but was always of the opinion that they were there watching him, unseen. He ordered the surveyors to ensure the men were never to be by themselves and they should always be armed. Surveyors would peer down their theodolites with pistols in their belts (Brooks, 1869, SLSA B11604).

Left: One of the 'double parties' at their camp (Brooks, 1869, SLSA B11601)

The small metal huts were the officers' quarters. They surrounded the government store, which had a half metal, half bark roof. When Goyder moved into his hut in April he said it was 'dreadfully hot—100° Fahrenheit from noon till 4 PM'. Later photographs show them being shaded by canvas or bark sheets. Until about July 1869, the store still has a portion of its roof made of bark sheets. Dr Peel's residence and surgery was in the lean-to at the end of the government store. (Brooks, 1869: *Top left*: SLSA B1153. *Left*: B1156. *Right*: B4647).

Above: A government well near Fort Point Camp known as '3 mile well', near Palmerston. The well is sheltered by a crude shade structure. '3 mile well' may have morphed into 3 mile dam in later years and, in which case, it was located near the modern Tiger Brennan Drive turn off to the suburb of Woolner (Sweet, 1869, SLSA B4651).

Left: Another view of the men at '3 mile well' (Brooks, 1869, SLSA B11602).

George Gailbraith MacLachlan was Goyder's nephew. He may be in this photograph of his camp, known as the Three Wells Camp, on the Howard River. MacLachlan stayed on in Darwin after the expedition, and was sent by Douglas to explore south-eastwards to the Roper River region, seeking overland telegraph routes. He discovered gold east of Pine Creek. He later surveyed the Roper River by boat and opened the 'river highway' up to Leichhardt's Bar, which was used as a depot point for the Overland Telegraph line. MacLachlan died of tuberculosis in 1873, aged 31 and is buried in the Goyder Road Cemetery in Darwin (Brooks, 1869, SLSA B9874).

Dr Robert Peel was invited to participate in the expedition as its medical officer and second in command. He was instrumental in starting the community entertainment activities, including the 'Theatre Royal'. Once Goyder left, on September 22, 1869, Peel remained in charge of the settlement. He was not a popular leader and was much criticised for his regular hunting and exploring trips, and his management of the alcohol supplies. By Christmas he was increasingly despondent about managing men who were bored, restless and forced to stay in Port Darwin for five months over the build-up and wet season because there was no ship to take them home. On New Year's Eve his roof was stoned by drunken revellers.

Above: Like many visitors he was happy to be photographed standing next to one of the north's ubiquitous giant termite mounds (Sweet, 1869, SLSA B43130).

Left: Dr Robert Peel (c1830–1894) (Anon., c1870, SLSA B925).

William Hoare was an English pharmacist who arrived in South Australia aboard the *Irene* in 1862. He was an eager recruit for Goyder's expedition in 1869 and was primarily the doctor's assistant, but he was also a skilled artist who painted numerous pictures of biological samples whose colours would have faded before reaching Adelaide. Goyder appended 39 of his paintings to his September dispatch, like this one of a fish, which he sent on the *Gulnare* with 34 cases of the skins of animals, Crustacea, coral, sponges, insects, fish, snakes and even live animals, collected by the naturalist Schultze. Hoare returned to Adelaide in 1870, and worked as a dispensing chemist but later emigrated to New Zealand. He returned to England about 1900. (Hoare, 1869, SLSA PGR 294/4/22)

Right: William Hoare (1841-1927), pharmacist, doctor's assistant and diarist, suffered from painful boils on his legs for most of the expedition (Anon., 1869, SLSA B926).

Left: One of Hoare's illustrations of fish.

Left: Men of the survey expedition in the bush near Port Darwin (Brooks 1869 (probably), SLSA, B60185).

Top right: An unidentified man sits with his rifle at the edge of a beach cliff, above a small cave. These caves are still a common sight along the beaches of the northern suburbs of Darwin (Brooks, 1869, SLSA B1144).

Right: In this photograph of an unidentified campsite, the windlass on the left stands above a well, and the men have been washing clothing. The man in the centre is armed with a carbine rifle (Brooks, 1869, SLSA B1140).

Left: The beach and the camp seen from a position on Fort Hill. Note the timber lean-to added to the end of the store. (Brooks, 1869, SLS B1154).

Centre: A view of the Fort Point camp taken from Fort Hill, showing the back of the store and the cookhouse with a stone chimney. A section of the store roof is still seen to be made of bark. (Brooks, 1869, SLSA B60184).

Right: The Fort Hill camp before the stables were built. The cookhouse is on the left. Two Aboriginal men talk with some of the expeditioners (Sweet, 1869, SLSA B4653).

The beach at Fort Point showing a boat with a seine fishing net for fishing, the *Gulnare*, and on the left, the *Midge's* boiler being used to desalinate water. Note the path at the base of Fort Hill. When settlers arrived in 1870, the ladies used to take an evening promenade around the hill (Sweet, 1869, SLSA B9749).

Left: Detail of the still. Charles Miller, the *Midge's* engineer could desalinate up to 150 gallons of water per day, using the Midge's boiler as a still (Sweet, 1869, SLSA B9749).

Goyder organised the surveyors into three teams he called 'double parties', because they were led by two first class surveyors: MacLachlan and McMinn; Smith and Harvey; and Woods and Mitchell. They were appointed separate areas starting from near Palmerston, and from the South Arm and East Arm of the harbour. Each double party of 32 men was divided into two single parties of 16 men. They were then split into groups of seven, with two left over as camp keepers or draftsmen. The work units were then allocated 33 square miles of land to survey each month. The work was tough and exhausting in the tropical heat and insects. They would regularly begin before dawn, by candlelight, and finish after dark. In this posed photograph, the second man from the left is thought to be the teamster Peter Krüss. If so, the other men may be members of Mitchell's survey party (Brooks, 1869, SLSA B1150).

Above: Fort Hill and the beach. Seven men pose in front of a shade shelter and boat. The *Gulnare* is visible, moored off Fort Hill (Sweet, 1869, SLSA B4649).

Left: The Point Fort camp in mid-1869. The long stable building is being constructed. The men are armed with rifles and pistols (Brooks, 1869, SLSA B1155).

These photos easily stitch together in a panorama of the Fort Point camp (and are used together on the cover of this book). They were taken in late August or early September, 1869, as the *Gulnare*, which returned on August 22, is moored off the point. It remained in Port Darwin until September 27, when Goyder and some of the party returned to Adelaide. The flag flew from Fort Hill near the grave of John Bennett and Richard Hazard. Fort Hill was removed completely in 1965 to make way for an iron ore port. Now it is the site of a new five star hotel (Sweet, 1869, SLSA *Left*: B4656 and *Right*: B4650).

Above: Arthur Smith's and William Harvey's survey teams at Southport (Sweet, 1869, SLSA B4655).

Left: Tumbling Waters on the River Blackmore. George Deane and George Bayfield pose on the rocks in the distance (Deane mentions being photographed in his diary). George Deane was a horse-tailer with a good education: he spoke French and he wrote well. He was engaged to George Bayfield's sister 'Ny'. Their marriage had to wait until 1870, as Deane was one of the 'volunteers' who stayed behind at Fort point after the survey was over (Sweet, 1869, SLSA B4654).

Above: Unidentified Fort Point staff pose in front of their tents, with the Palmerston Plateau (where the Government Residency was later built) in the background. The man on the right is standing next to the barrel which is collecting desalinated water from the long cooling pipe behind him (Brooks, 1869, SLSA B1151).

Right: The Fort Point camp with men working on the roads. John Bennett's grave, which was completed in August 1869, can be seen at the top of Fort Hill (Brooks, 1869, SLSA B1152).

Above: After the surveying was complete the teams were set to improving the roadway up to the plateau where Palmerston was to be built. Many of the men were not happy with this new line of work and what was arguably the Northern Territory's first strike was held on December 28, 1869, when the men demanded a holiday to celebrate 12 months since their departure from Adelaide. The roads are now known as Hughes Avenue (upper) and Kitchener Drive (lower) (photo dated 1869–1870, SLSA B1866).

Left: Doctor's Gully, and Peel's Well, proved to be a reliable water source for the settlement. William Hayes started a garden there within a few days of arrival. He was aided by Robert Burton, Frank Hood and Ned Tuckwell, who returned from an expedition to the defunct Escape Cliffs settlement, on March 18, with banana palms, arrowroot, and other plants. The banana plants and sugar cane that grow behind a fence in this photo are mature and this suggests the photo was taken either in late 1869 (before September 22) or in 1870 (Sweet c1869/70, SLSA B17389/4).

An overlay map showing the site of Goyder's camp and modern development. The long rectangular building was the stables and the shorter one, the government store. The overlay comes from a survey by DD Daly with MacLachlan's signature in 1869. It overlays a contemporary photograph (ref: NT Archives Service, Department of Infrastructure Planning and Logistics, Survey, Goyder's Camp, 1869).

Above: Many of the expedition pose for this photograph beside the new stables, probably in September 1869. George Goyder was a very small man. It is possible that the small man on the left is him (see detail enlargement) (Sweet, 1869, SLSA B4652).

Right: Detail of the men: could this be George Goyder? (Sweet, 1869, SLSA B4652).

Above: Ned Tuckwell's government carpentry workshop and boat shed on the beach, constructed from the combination of wooden poles and a tin roof. A wooden rowing boat sits outside the boat shed. The seated man is thought to be Ned Tuckwell, who remained behind in Palmerston after the settlers arrived in 1870. He was joined by his wife, Eliza, and their four children. Ned died in 1882 and is buried in the Goyder Road cemetery in Darwin (Sweet, c1870, SLSA B9741).

Right: The Fort Point camp as seen from the rocky beach in August or September (Sweet, 1869, SLSA B9748).

A view of Fort Hill from the plateau, with the *Gulnare* moored in the harbour (Sweet, 1869, SLSA B4648).

Also by Derek Pugh

DARWIN 1869 The Second Northern Territory Expedition

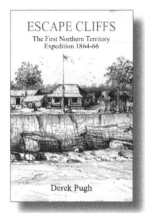

Darwin, the unique and vibrant city in Australia's tropical north, was almost stillborn.

The Northern Territory had its beginnings under the governance of South Australia. Land was sold to investors, unseen and unsurveyed and in an unknown location. The sales raised the funds needed to found the new colony of Palmerston, the future capital of the Northern Territory of South Australia. The First Northern Territory Expedition was sent north to make it a reality. But, it failed miserably and the government faced huge losses and insufficient reserves to refund its investors.

To mitigate the loss, a new venture was envisaged— The Second Northern Territory Expedition—and there was only one man thought capable of ensuring a successful survey of the north: the Surveyor General, George Woodroffe Goyder.

Goyder was an extraordinary man, full of frenetic energy and with a phenomenal work ethic. The survey took him and his expert teams of surveyors and bushmen only eight months. It resulted in the laying out of the city of Palmerston (now called Darwin), three rural towns and hundreds of rural blocks spreading over almost 270,000 hectares, all pegged out in the bush and mapped. The blocks were carved out of Larrakia and Wulna lands—without permission or compensation—and conflict with the Aborigines was an ever-present danger. Two men were speared—one fatally.

Darwin grew from these somewhat humble but tumultuous beginnings. It was the only pre-Federation Australian capital established late enough to be photographed from its first settlement, and it is a survivor of challenges and privations unheard of in more temperate climes.

Darwin's story is written on its maps. Street names such as Knuckey, McLachlan, Daly, Woods, Bennett, Harvey and Smith Streets, recall the surveyors and their teams. Suburbs such as Millner, Larrakeyah, Bellamack and Stuart Park remind us of the city's earliest days. It is the story of how the courage and diligence of a few led to the founding of the city we know today.

ESCAPE CLIFFS The First Northern Territory Expedition 1864–66

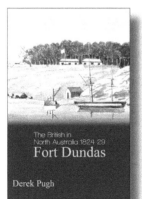

This is a true story of greed, courage, exploration, murder, wasted efforts, life and death struggles, insubordination, incredible seamanship, and extraordinary bushmanship, amid government bungling and Aboriginal resistance, during South Australia's first attempt at colonising their Northern Territory in 1864.

The South Australians wanted their state to be the premier state of Australia. The new settlement was expected to open up a trading route across the country to Asia and beyond, and exploit the agricultural and mining opportunities of the interior. It was to be at no cost to the taxpayer, as the land was sold, unseen and unsurveyed, to investors in Adelaide and London, prior to the First Northern Territory Expedition even setting out. The investors were already calculating their returns, but then, as the saying goes, the fight really started …

"A fantastic read: insightful, cohesive, sequential, and well-paced. Loved it. Plenty of photos and maps to set the scene, with the addition of well-researched, complementary, first-hand accounts and primary records. Pugh has captured the essence of the time, place and characters: their personalities, hardships, successes and celebrations. I wanted to read it to find out what was going to happen next. Pugh's writing style is 'alive' and easy to read." Jill Finch.

The British in North Australia 1824–29 FORT DUNDAS

Fort Dundas was the first of a series of fortified locations around the coast of Australia.

Its purpose was twofold. First, it was a physical demonstration of Britain's claim to the New Holland continent. Second, it was the start of a British trading post that would become a second Singapore and compete with Batavia.

The settlement was named in a ceremony on October 21, 1824 but it was not a success. In its short existence, we have tales of suffering, survival, greed, piracy, slavery, murder, kidnapping, scurvy, and battles with the Indigenous inhabitants of the islands, the Tiwi. And also, the first European wedding and the birth of the first European children in northern Australia occurred on the island.

The settlement left behind 34 dead—victims of disease, poor diet and Tiwi spears. Others died when the crews of the fort's supply ships were slaughtered and beheaded by Malay pirates on islands to the north. Two cabin boys were enslaved by the pirates.

What happened at Fort Dundas and why it was abandoned has been largely untold. Nevertheless, it is one of the most engaging stories of nineteenth-century Australia, presented here in Derek Pugh's usual captivating style.

Printed in Australia
AUOW01n1927170918
302872AU00004B/4